TOP TIPS
for
LIFE

For more than four years, the @TwopTwips Twitter account has been spewing forth ridiculous yet ingenious gobbets of advice to its thousands of loyal followers, often causing them to involuntarily snort with laughter on commuter trains whilst fellow passengers tut and shake their heads. Those fellow passengers are missing out. It is one of the highest-followed non-celebrity Twitter accounts in the UK, and *The Times Magazine* placed @TwopTwips sixth in its list of the funniest tweeters in the English-speaking world.

David Harris is the curator of @TwopTwips, as well as working for popular humour website The Poke.

from TWOP TWIPS

TOP TIPS *for* LIFE

COMPLETELY USELESS ADVICE FOR MODERN LIVING

COMPILED BY DAVID HARRIS

EBURY PRESS

1 3 5 7 9 10 8 6 4 2

Published in 2014 by Ebury Press, an imprint of Ebury Publishing
A Random House Group company

Copyright © David Harris 2014

David Harris has asserted his right to be identified as the author of this Work in
accordance with the Copyright, Designs and Patents Act 1988

Illustrations by BeCk Cartoons. www.cartooned.at

The Random House Group Limited Reg. No. 954009

Addresses for companies within the Random House Group can be found at
www.randomhouse.co.uk

A CIP catalogue record for this book is available from the British Library

The Random House Group Limited supports the Forest Stewardship
Council® (FSC®), the leading international forest-certification organisation.
Our books carrying the FSC label are printed on FSC®-certified paper. FSC is
the only forest-certification scheme supported by the leading environmental
organisations, including Greenpeace. Our paper procurement policy can be
found at www.randomhouse.co.uk/environment

MIX
Paper from
responsible sources
FSC® C016897

Designed and set by seagulls.net

Printed and bound by CPI Group (UK) Ltd, Croydon, CR0 4YY

ISBN 9780091959944

To buy books by your favourite authors and register for offers visit
www.randomhouse.co.uk

This book is dedicated to its many contributors on Twitter, without whom it would just be a book full of nowt. Thank you.

TOP TIPS FOR LIFE

FOR FUN, when visiting friends, teach your
two-year-old to point into empty rooms
and say, 'Who is that sad little boy?'

@ realrossnoble

COMMUTERS. Convince passing traffic you were
on *Come Dine With Me* by riding a black cab home
and holding up laminated numbers.

@ MOBHANDED

AVOID the hassle of making toast in the morning
by leaving a slice of bread on the radiator
overnight. Simply get up at 4am to 'turn'.

@ Birdflaps

FAMILIES. Save on costly caravan holidays
by arguing in one room and then
sleeping in a cupboard.

@ AbbeyBloom

RECREATE the Wimbledon Ladies' Final at home
by putting your cat's tail under a rocking chair.

@ DesKellyDM

TWOP TWIPS

CHINA SHOPS. Avoid your worst nightmare by simply installing a cattle grid to your entrance.

@ JCautomatic

SNOW. For more media coverage ensure you focus on London and the South East.

@ martingower

ANNOY MC Hammer by going to a museum with him, pointing at every exhibit and asking 'Can I touch this?'

@ GlennyRodge

PRETEND to be on *Blind Date* by standing in a train toilet, opening the electric door and smiling shyly at a waiting passenger.

@ mrneilforsyth

SURPRISE your hamster by smashing through the door of his plastic house at 5am with a cocktail sausage shouting 'Police!'

@ buschenfeld

TOP TIPS FOR LIFE

FIND OUT how loud your partner can scream by waking them up on an aeroplane flight wearing your life jacket and oxygen mask.

@ vinharris

LIVEN up a trip to the supermarket by mischievously dropping a pregnancy test into couples' trolleys when they're not looking.

@ pandamoanimum

PAINT your house number on your bin to make it easier for binmen to leave it outside the wrong address.

@ wallaceme

CONVINCE your wife you work for Ocado by coming home in the wrong clothes, with the wrong briefcase and with someone else's wife.

@ Castaignede

MOBILITY SCOOTER DRIVERS. Attach a string of bananas behind your vehicle for that exciting Mario Kart look.

@ _woz_

TWOP TWIPS

HELP fellow commuters by googling the book
they're reading and telling them the ending,
thus saving them valuable time.

@ loop_deleted

SAVE MONEY on phone sex lines by texting
filth to your landline and have the BT woman
read it to you at a fraction of the cost.

@ BroomOwl

FULFIL a lifetime's ambition to swim with dolphins
by emptying a can of Value tuna in the bath.

@ Johnny_Two_Dogs

SINGLE CATS. Looking to find a partner?
Simply log into my Facebook and select a mate
from the hundreds of photos in my news feed.

@ jojubs

INSOMNIACS. Use those bonus night-time hours
to think about your problems and fears.

@ pfon73

CREATE your own Amazon Kindle by reading a book through the window.

K C E B

TWOP TWIPS

RELIVE that glorious 'just left school forever'
feeling by deleting your Facebook account.

@ TartanCrusader

HOSPITALS. Change 'A&E' to 'A 'n' E' for a more
informal-sounding emergency department.

@ Jon_Hopkins_

OFFCUTS from lighthouse carpets make ideal
surrounds for inflatable paddling pools.

@ rowzed

FLY TIP the contents of your home PC's recycle
bin by dumping it on a computer at the
local library via a USB stick.

@ BobWriggles

MAN-SIZE Kleenex can also be used
for blowing your nose.

@ SteveSparshott

TOP TIPS FOR LIFE

ASKING Jedward for their autographs should
be enough of a distraction for you to be
able to bite one of them in the face.

@ lee107

SHOPKEEPERS. Give your customers the 24-hour
garage experience by doubling your prices and
serving them through your letterbox.

@ timcore

OBITUARY pages in local papers often act as
a preview for upcoming job openings.

@ iamnotniles

SAVE on expensive patio heaters by simply
staying indoors when it is cold and dark.

@ Raspberryuke

FOR FREE WiFi on the move simply drive
alongside a National Express coach.

@ Mark_Collinge

TWOP TWIPS

A SUREFIRE cure for listlessness is to write down the possible causes, one after the other, on a piece of paper.

@ benald

EMERGENCY SERVICES. Reduce hoax 999 calls by simply changing your number to one that's more difficult to remember.

@ 5fendle

SANTA. Avoid the hassle of delivering presents by leaving a card and getting children to pick them up from the depot.

@ orangeaurochs

A LADDER, turned upside-down, can be used for climbing down off things.

@ doctorcamel

AN INSOMNIAC bagpipe player with amoebic dysentery makes an inexpensive baby for childless couples.

@ mothmun

CHEER up children by telling them that their broken Easter eggs are just 'scrambled'.

TWOP TWIPS

TRICK your cat into thinking it's been spiked with LSD by building a replica of your kitchen on the other side of the cat flap.

@ Bromptonite

OLD PEOPLE. Save time by asking for things in sixes instead of 'a half dozen'.

@ ortidog

STOP your children from looking at inappropriate internet sites by posting naked pictures of their mum on them.

@ mothmun

MEN. Avoid the hassle of visiting rubbish dumps by placing unwanted items in your garage until you die.

@ JCautomatic

NEVER buy an iPad in the street from a man who's out of breath.

@ Lambandflag

TOP TIPS FOR LIFE

BECOME an unpaid, on-call IT support person by letting your neighbours know you 'work in computers a bit'.

@ Bromptonite

SCIENTISTS. Give a 'religious feel' to your conclusions by not showing your working.

@ ClintJEdwards

CDs make the perfect vanity mirror for women who don't like their noses.

@ adambloomie2

PRETEND to be Robert Peston by reading from the *Financial Times* whilst straining to take a poo.

@ RandomVitriol

MEN. Trick your wife that you've been hypnotised by shouting 'Cockadoodledoo!' and running to the pub whenever she says 'housework'.

@ _woz_

GLUING all of your possessions together will make it hard for an intruder to get them out through a door or window.

@ RichNeville

RIHANNA fans. For the ultimate tribute have triplets and call each child 'Ella'.

@ Oak411

GPs. A bowl of apples in your waiting room will allow you more time to play golf or to self-medicate with morphine.

@ GreatHeckBrew

A FRAMED photo of yourself brushing your hair or having a shave saves the expense of costly mirrors in the bathroom.

@ FutureDave

CONVINCE people you can expertly play the bagpipes by picking up a set of bagpipes and having a stab at it.

@ _woz_

AVOID the 'butter side down' scenario by
dropping your toast, and then buttering it.

B з c K

@ MaudTheMaid

CONVINCE people you're a psychologist by nodding and stroking your chin while they talk, then claiming they fancy their mum.

@ Mullies

AVOID having to do a best man speech by simply alienating all your friends at a young age.

@ slimtim70

AGGRESSIVE DOGS. By snarling and barking less, people will be more likely to move closer to you, making them easier to bite.

@ yearsofpractice

MARGARINE smeared around the inside of the toilet bowl prevents unsightly skid marks. Re-apply every 3 or 4 flushes.

@ FutureDave

TEACHERS. Bring the Nativity play up to date with a 'Jeremy Kyle style' DNA test while God and Joseph await the results.

@ Johnny_Two_Dogs

TOP TIPS FOR LIFE

RECREATE the Wacky Warehouse experience at home by sitting at the dining table with your kids' shoes while they jump on the sofa.

@ jerowney

CHOOSING a gift for a friend from Norfolk? Always buy mittens and not gloves to prevent one of those 'awkward moments'.

@ Booneyboone

GO DOGGING whilst dressed as a traffic warden. All the sexy fun with none of the shame.

@ Philwalkercomic

BIRDS. Stand closer together at dawn. That way you won't have to shout.

@ TheBathBird

DON'T waste money on expensive sat navs. Simply order a taxi to your desired destination and follow it in your car.

@ FutureDave

TWOP TWIPS

GIVE the impression that a relative has died by taking all your family to a local working men's club any weekday afternoon.

@ Mr_R1cardo

LONELY PEOPLE. Cover your bed in coats to make it feel like you're at a house party.

@ Biltawulf

MOTORISTS. Thumbing through the road atlas takes up precious time. Simply move to the area featured on the cover.

@ kgillard

MAKE your neighbours splash urine all over themselves by putting clingfilm over your letterbox.

@ RichNeville

AVOID the annoyance of having to wait for energy-saving lightbulbs to warm up by simply leaving them switched on all the time.

@ deaneager

CONVINCE callers to your house that you are definitely not in by standing completely still when the call goes to answer phone.

ƃ ɔ ∃ ꓘ

TWOP TWIPS

JOCKEYS. Riding a unicorn instead of a horse could make all the difference in a photo finish.

@ NotReallyNathan

CONVINCE people you are Michael McIntyre by nodding a lot and noticing things.

@ kbutler88

WOMEN. Avoid the hassle and expense of hair straighteners by simply not eating your crusts.

@ Johnny_Two_Dogs

DOCTORS. When testing reflexes a claw hammer swung at the face works better than a toffee hammer on the knee.

@ JCautomatic

LOOKING at the people queuing in Greggs is a quick and easy way to boost your self-esteem.

@ amateursuman

TOP TIPS FOR LIFE

IF FINDING yourself too calm or relaxed in any situation, just count down from 10 in your head.

@ bobbobob

FOOL a complete stranger that you've arrived home OK by ringing a random number three times.

@ Mr_R1cardo

ENLIVEN a dull event such as a board meeting or funeral with a 'pile on'.

@ SteveSparshott

ARACHNOPHOBES. Reduce your anxiety over spiders by picturing them on the toilet.

@ Johnny_Two_Dogs

FOOL cats into thinking their dinner is ready by using a fork to bang on a tin of baked beans.

@ JonathanOB_

TWOP TWIPS

GIRLS. Waving your fingers in front of
your face stops you from crying.

@ silveraudi2

TRICK old people into thinking they are
haunted by the ghost of Thora Hird by
turning their stairlift on and hiding.

@ Bromptonite

FALL DOWN the stairs whilst holding a guitar. Hey
presto, you've just written a Pete Doherty song.

@ theUKdude

FOOL your dog into thinking you've gone
on holiday by putting him in the
kennels for a fortnight.

@ milesey70

iPAD USERS. Stick a photograph of your
face on the back of your iPad so your family
don't forget what you look like.

@ doubledrat63

TOP TIPS FOR LIFE

OLD PEOPLE. Avoid falling off the
motorway by simply driving slowly
and staying in the middle lane.

@ NorthEastCorner

TENNIS FANS. Pretend you're at
Wimbledon by laughing and clapping
every time a pigeon lands on your lawn.

@ IHPower

STOP your dog from pulling on its lead
by walking a bit faster.

@ JCAutomatic

PRETEND you are talking to an evil twin in jail
by holding an old phone and talking to
yourself in the bathroom mirror.

@ darrenhoskins

CREATE your own groundbreaking new cop
drama by simply dubbing old episodes of
NYPD Blue into Norwegian or whatever.

@ pfon73

CAR ALARM MAKERS. Add a silent 'vibrate only' mode for night-time use.

@ aderixon

UK GOVERNMENT. Save us lots of tedious scrolling by rebranding as 'aaaUnited Kingdom'.

@ ian_ec1

PET OWNERS. Maintain a frosty relationship with your pet to avoid being sad when it dies.

@ mrneilforsyth

ROAD WORKERS Why not have Formal Friday? Wear a suit and sit around drinking Earl Grey all day.

@ SteveSparshott

FILM LOVERS. Replicate the Transformers films by reading *Nuts* magazine whilst someone lets off fireworks in your face.

@ TonyCowards

CAT OWNERS calculate your weight by weighing yourself whilst holding your cat, then weigh your cat and deduct from total.

@ hodgo34

TWOP TWIPS

LE TOUR ORGANISERS. Make it easier for the cyclists by moving it to Holland where it's flat and drugs are widely available.

@ fletcherchriss

TRICK the old into thinking you're a close relative by regularly turning up for dinner and getting them to babysit at weekends.

@ DAVE_RoCK

MEN. Acquire instant forgiveness for any kind of appalling behaviour by simply telling people that you are 'teething'.

@ capnbobfrapples

NEW BUSINESSES. Convince potential customers that you know what you are doing by including 'solutions' in your company name.

@ Col_Turner

TEENS. Remove and save vowels from everyday texts so that you may use them later in life as long, low groans.

@ redpola

TOP TIPS FOR LIFE

INFLATE your whoopee cushion with
actual farts for added authenticity.

@ FrankieMcGinty

SAVE the blushes of someone who has fallen
over in the street by lying down next to them
and pretending it's a protest.

@ StevoGDC

GET VALUE for money from your Stannah stairlift
by buying it in your early 30s.

@ country_vince

DENTISTS. Don't go on telly recommending
brands of toothpaste. Think of future business:
recommend Skittles instead.

@ mr_njk

GIVE meetings a parliamentary feel by simply
shouting 'blurghyhlghygh' when you agree or
disagree with anything someone says.

@ pacific_amnesia

TWOP TWIPS

ATTENTION-SEEKERS. Use Facebook to write vague, enigmatic status updates which will prompt responses like 'u ok hun? X'

@ craiguito

ANTHROPOLOGISTS. Study the 'fight or flight' response in Homo sapiens at the Birmingham International Ryanair check-in.

@ alienonline

SAVE money on gravy this Christmas by simply serving everyone half the amount and calling it jus.

@ alanshoesmith

UNSURE whether you've loaded everything to be washed into the machine? Simply press the START button to confirm you haven't.

@ bigajm

LADIES. Save money on expensive high heels by simply walking around everywhere on tiptoes.

@ ohdannyboy

INSTANTLY wipe your child's memory of the day by simply asking them what they did at school.

ʞɔɐꓭ

TWOP TWIPS

PRETEND a nuclear bomb has been dropped on Paris by simply going to Blackpool.

@ JCautomatic

ENSURE your wife has an authentic shopping experience while online by standing a foot behind her and looking at your phone.

@ RANTINGMALE

CONVINCE PEOPLE you own an iPad by drawing a picture of the internet on your Etch A Sketch.

@ mothmun

RECREATE the experience of Ikea on a Saturday by going to a football match with a supermarket trolley.

@ craiguito

TAXI DRIVERS. Copy theme parks by offering punters photos of themselves taken during the ride as they exit your cab.

@ deaneager

TOP TIPS FOR LIFE

PRETEND to be a community support officer
by pretending to be a police officer.

@ mrneilforsyth

USE PVA glue and dried lentils
for a hippy vajazzle effect.

@ supernoodle76

ELECTRONIC cigarettes make a handy
and safe Christmas present for children
wanting to learn to smoke.

@ chipshopforks

ENVIRONMENTALISTS. Be careful when car
sharing. I took a neighbour's car to go
shopping and he was bloody livid.

@ _b_4

RECREATE the thrill of a drunken
night out by simply texting an
ex-girlfriend with one eye closed.

@ JCautomatic

AMERICAN DETECTIVES. The week before
your partner of 20 years retires is an
ideal time for some annual leave.

@ RANTINGMALE

AVOID an embarrassing photocopier incident
at your work Xmas party by having a business
document tattooed to your arse.

@ Pundamentalism

SAVE your wife buying expensive fishnet tights
by looking at her legs through a sieve.

@ mrneilforsyth

FOOTBALLERS. Rather than hug your team-mate
when he scores, why not do it when he makes a
mistake? He probably needs it more.

@ GlennyRodge

SPOIL burglars' fun by pooing in every room
of your house before going on holiday.

@ 664NOTB

HOLDING a chin under someone's chin is a great way of finding out if they like a chin under their chin.

TELLING a pal 'your baby's so cute, are you sure
it's yours?' is a subtle and amusing way
of implying his wife's a slag.

@ sixthformpoet

iPHONE ADULTERERS. Store your mistress's
name as '20% Low Battery' in your phone.

@ johnholtmagic

GET the feeling that you've spent a week in
Carlisle by spending an afternoon in Carlisle.

@ timcore

LIGHTEN the mood if you are ever in a car crash
by filling your air-bags with confetti today.

@ DavieLegend

SAVE money on expensive umbrellas by
constructing shelters from building materials
and staying inside them when it rains.

@ _L_M_C_

TOP TIPS FOR LIFE

TRAPPED WIND? A quick trip on public transport appears to provide relief.

PRACTISE spectating at Wimbledon by walking down the centre aisle of Tesco's looking for your wife.

LADIES. Find out what your husband really wants for Christmas by checking his browser history.

PRETEND you are on *Total Wipeout* by crawling through your local carwash.

THWART potential biographers by living a mundane and insignificant life, never aspiring to anything above mediocrity.

TWOP TWIPS

A BUILDERS' PORTALOO makes an ideal
Tardis for strong-stomached kids.

@ gdorean

OAPs. Phone doesn't ring as often these days?
Pop a 'How's My Driving?' sticker on your
car for hours of 'lively' chat.

@ Johnny_Two_Dogs

TIME MACHINE owners. Type in Canada,
Summer, 1969, and prevent all boys
called Bryan from buying a guitar.

@ _Enanem_

BEFORE you close a web page make sure
you scroll up to the top so it's in the
right position for the next person.

@ amateuradam

SAVE money on Peter Kay tickets by
just thinking about the old days.

@ vinharris

CHANGE any love song into a sea shanty by simply replacing the word 'baby' with 'matey'.

@ alicejupp

ASPIRING celebrities. Combine buying lunch with the excitement of being interviewed by going to Subway.

@ thomassays

SIRI. When unable to understand the Scottish accent, have an educated guess by recommending the nearest public house.

@ GazWeetman

REMIND yourself why you've never arranged a school reunion by logging into Facebook.

@ RANTINGMALE

COLDPLAY. Recreate the success of Steps by splitting up now and reforming in ten years when, with a spot of luck, I'll be dead.

@ Booneyboone

CONFUSE the Google Street View car by running alongside it dressed as a house.

@ scottywrotem

CREATE your own miniature 'Dalek Bride' by sticking a nail into a shuttlecock.

@ pavanwar

TRICK people into thinking you're a time traveller by buying clothes in Middlesbrough.

@ Bromptonite

DUMP your recyclable bottles on other countries by putting written pleasantries in them and throwing them into the sea.

@ daryllayton

SAVE money on spray tans by simply zipping yourself in a tent with a 3 year old and a multipack of Wotsits.

@ JCautomatic

CRYING in the shower because you're so lonely is a great way to save money on tissues.

TWOP TWIPS

TAKE the first half of your postcode and add the second half of your car registration number to create your robot porn star name.

@ brightom

GIVE house guests an authentic Ikea experience by making them walk through every room on the way out.

@ Bromptonite

SAVE money on expensive Quorn sausages by simply filling condoms with the contents of a hoover bag.

@ Sefty101

DRIVERS. Ensure you never fall asleep on a long journey by carefully trapping a bit of your hair in the sunroof.

@ vinharris

LISTENING to 'Wonderful Christmastime' by Paul McCartney will soon get you in the mood for January.

@ npellinacci

TOP TIPS FOR LIFE

EXPERIENCE a quiet Sunday morning
with a toddler by putting your head in
a tumble dryer full of spanners.

@ moanup

WRITING 'Tease Me' on a Viagra makes
an ideal Love Heart substitute for a
partner with erectile problems.

@ IrnMnky

A PLASTIC carrier bag is an ideal alternative
to wrapping paper this Christmas for those
who simply can't be arsed.

@ mickypne

THIS winter, hide a collection of bones
in your snowman as a surprise for the
children when it melts.

@ MooseAllain

CALL OF DUTY GAMERS. Temporarily blind and
disorientate your opponent by unexpectedly
ripping open his bedroom curtains.

@ tommillard

SOLUBLE ASPIRIN make a brilliant bath bomb
when pampering your hamster.
@ parkes7

HERBAL SLEEPING PILLS are ideal for anyone
without even the slightest problem sleeping.
@ eddieunwin

CHECK if your co-workers are cyborgs
by lunging at them suddenly with a USB stick
with the top off. Then observe reactions.
@ petermcgladdery

RECREATE the thrill of shopping at Hollister by
trying on a child's T-shirt with the lights off.
@ HoracioMelvin

SURPRISE Dad this Father's Day by
knocking on his door after 15 years.
@ StillTheBigOJ

REVISIT your youth of ringing doorbells and running away by becoming a DHL delivery driver.

CHILDREN. Poking your tongue out of the side of your mouth when cutting with plastic scissors actually makes them sharper.

@ SilverTyne

GIVE your wife an authentic fairground experience at home by leering at her whilst spinning her on an office chair.

@ ItsTomKing

STUART PEARCE. Adult haircuts are available for only one pound extra.

@ EdwardBowden

FLAT DWELLERS. Convince your downstairs neighbours you're learning to juggle by occasionally banging the floor three times.

@ cv19777

A MIXTURE of Skittles and M&Ms make an ideal gift for a kinky sweet-toothed relative.

@ Scotty_McTweety

TOP TIPS FOR LIFE

DOG OWNERS. Save money on water bills by defecating with your pet on the daily walk and poop-scooping both together.

@ Remo26599

SQUASH PLAYERS. Don't waste money on two racquets. Simply take your hit and pass the racquet on to your opponent.

@ JayLagan

CONVINCE your friends that they are ghosts by ignoring them and carving their names into park benches.

@ alasdoug

WHEN near venomous snakes, try walking on your hands as statistically most people get bitten on the feet or legs.

@ 5fendle

CRIMINALS. Avoid 'requesting that a further 9 offences be taken into consideration'. If anything, ask that they be ignored.

@ gomark

NELLY FURTADO. Back up your 'I'm like a bird' claims by defecating on a statue or eating sick off the street.

@ HoracioMelvin

SIMULATE alien abduction by scrolling out from your location on Google Street View with a finger up your bum.

@ QuantumPirate

CYCLISTS. The hollowed-out skin of a freshly baked jacket potato makes an ideal testicle warmer for chilly autumn mornings.

@ Bromptonite

RECREATE the excitement of a game of Space Invaders by throwing apples at a line-dancing convention.

@ death_stairs

SAVE money on laundry bills by dressing your used crockery in your dirty pants and socks before putting it in the dishwasher.

@ MooseAllain

@ therealflannerz

TWOP TWIPS

HELP the birds find food this winter
by printing out a map showing the route
to Africa, and leaving it in the window.

@ ThisLeeNoble

ALWAYS keep a pair of crutches by the side
of the sofa. A ready excuse for a messy house
when you get unexpected visitors.

@ Trudski2012

PREVENT your bins from blowing away
in windy conditions by weighing them down
with unwanted household items.

@ MONKFISHooo

LEE EVANS fans. Unable to attend one
of his gigs? Simply blow up a large balloon
and let it go in your living room.

@ BigWoodenSpoon

CONVINCE fellow drivers you were a budgie in a
previous life by pecking at your rear view mirror.

@ Wytchfinder_Gen

TOP TIPS FOR LIFE

CREMATORIUM OWNERS. Provide a welcoming environment whilst offsetting fuel bills by offering mourners baked potatoes etc.

@ JonnyB

IMMUNISE your children the natural way by allowing them to play on a Wetherspoon's fruit machine for ten minutes.

@ superluckytiger

CONSOLIDATE all of your blinks into an hour and a half lie-in, thus preventing you from missing anything throughout the day.

@ drifterpowell

LONELY bald men. Why not get a tattoo on the back of your head that reads 'How's My Walking?' and add your phone number.

@ tokyo_sexwhale

RECREATE watching *Celebrity Big Brother* in 3D by walking into a pub and not recognising anyone.

@ jojubs

EASILY remove a red wine stain from
your carpet by setting fire to the house.

@ RANTINGMALE

LOST your chopping board? Download a marble
background for your iPad. Hey presto!

@ lightng

GET free clothes by the end of the week
by posting yellow bin bags marked 'Friday'
through a neighbour's letterbox.

@ gdorean

CREATE your own Jodie Marsh action figure
by simply filling a condom with Maltesers.

@ ChribHibble

BLUES MUSICIANS. Invest in an alarm clock
with a snooze button then you can
write two songs that day.

@ QuintinForbes

SCREW TOPS from tomato purée tubes
make ideal fezzes for Turkish hamsters.

COMMUTERS. Get that real limousine experience at a fraction of the cost by drinking Lambrini at the back of the bus.

@ hu_is_who

BUY your cat a scratch post so it has something to walk past on the way to destroying your sofa.

@ miguelmerry

STRUGGLING to get your children's attention? Simply sit down in front of the TV looking comfortable.

@ Thuckster69

LEARN a lesson from toast. Before going out drinking, why not butter the back of your head so that you don't fall on your face?

@ ChribHibble

AUDI DRIVERS. Save money on wing mirrors by simply getting close enough to use the ones on the car in front.

TOP TIPS FOR LIFE

@ miguelmerry

GAMBLING ADDICTS. Recreate the thrill of being surrounded by disappointed faces and small pens by visiting your local Argos.

@ jameswrees

CALENDAR MAKERS. In leap years scrap the miserable 29th February in favour of a 32nd July. Hey presto, extra day of summer.

@ jemward

TEACH your child about the importance of punctuation by making them some 'No, More Tears' shampoo out of lemon juice and vinegar.

@ gazhaman

LIVEN up being a parent by pretending your baby runs a drug gang and his monitor is 'the wire' you are using to gather evidence.

@ iamreddave

PRETEND you're a guest on *The One Show* by sitting on a sofa for 30 minutes and watching *The One Show*.

@ MattSolly

GP SURGERIES. Create more business by providing a waiting-room touch screen for all the ill people to share their infections.

@ ollieclark

SAVE time when meeting a person who says 'you'll either love me or hate me' by always deciding to hate them.

@ hammyfry

MALE PORN STARS. Supplement your income by qualifying as a plumber or fridge technician.

@ Pundamentalism

DISCOVER the exact age of an old person simply by standing next to them at a bus stop.

@ GlennyRodge

IMPROVE your chances of getting a loan from the bank by proving to them that you don't need it.

@ Thuckster

TEMPS. The best way to remember all your co-workers' names is by eating their food in the fridge.

@vinharris

TWOP TWIPS

FUSSY EATERS. A fried egg makes an ideal gluten- and lactose-free pancake.

@ GinBroguesHats

DARREN DAY. Changing your first name to 'Pancake' will ensure at least one day of fame a year.

@ vinharris

CREATE your own Florence & The Machine album by locking an owl in a wind chime shop.

@ sixft2blue

THWART nicotine cravings by smoking cigarettes at regular intervals throughout the day.

@ 5fendle

BAKERS and toaster makers. Get together and decide what size a slice of bread should be and stick to it.

@ ThisLeeNoble

TOP TIPS FOR LIFE

THE QUEEN. You've had the same job for
60 years now with a good track record.
Why not apply for a promotion?

@ GinBroguesHats

LORD SUGAR. Save your time and ours by
hiring a recruitment consultancy to vet
potential *Apprentice* candidates.

@ GinBroguesHats

POLITELY inform friends that you're going for
a dump by asking for their WiFi password
before going to the bathroom.

@ Pundamentalism

PREPARE your children for office life by acting
awkwardly around them in the kitchen.

@ superluckytiger

RELIVE that Ryanair experience by getting mates
to flog you scratchcards through a megaphone
while you're trying to sleep.

@ NickMotown

TWOP TWIPS

MAKE toast seem more exciting by
pretending you've rescued a slice of
bread from a burning building.

@ MooseAllain

ANNOY Jehovah's Witnesses by ignoring them
whenever they try to tell you a knock knock joke.

@ jbrownridge

MARRIED MEN. Cheer up your wife at social
events by introducing her as your 'ex-girlfriend'.

@ NickMotown

GET involved in a big game of hide and seek
by becoming a member of staff at B&Q.

@ lcrompton2810

RECREATE the illicit thrill of an office affair by
having sex with your wife in a PC World.

@ superluckytiger

DOUBLE the excitement of watching Formula 1 by doing the ironing at the same time.

TWOP TWIPS

FIRST CLASS stamps make excellent
posters for patriotic ants.

@ robotattack

HOMEOPATHS. Save money on petrol by filling
up at the water pump. Your car will remember
the petrol from the previous fill.

@ daveaddey

TENPIN BOWLERS. Make your second shot
easier by deliberately missing your first.

@ sidlowe

IF YOU'RE feeling low and need a bit of an ego
boost, have a read through your eBay feedback.
Turns out I'm pretty amazing.

@ thejuice78

FOR those who missed Ed Sheeran on last
night's Brits, worry not: there is a squashed
fox on the A470 just outside Cardiff.

@ king_morg

TOP TIPS FOR LIFE

ENJOY knowing that your partner is having a
good night's sleep by listening to them snore.

@ Cosworthlady

BANKS. Consolidate two security questions into
one by asking customers for their porn star name.

@ GarrLyons

OLD PEOPLE. Identify yourself as a
hazard to other road users by means of
a panama hat on the parcel shelf.

@ djfox67

CREATE a home-made pregnancy test by
waiting 18 years then measuring how much
resentment is coming towards you.

@ salcoops

COVERING someone's eyes and saying
'Guess who?' is a really fun way to
make friends at urinals.

@ DannyDutch

TWOP TWIPS

CIRCUMVENT a hosepipe ban by holding
a riot in your garden, causing the police
to use a water cannon.

@ IAmSimonHarris

PENSIONERS. Take a cue from penguins by
huddling together to keep warm and sliding
down the High Street on your belly.

@ antinbath

STAND next to someone doing press-ups.
Hey presto! You're a personal trainer.

@ DougJNicholls

DON'T waste money on expensive pets, simply
live in absolute squalor and let them come to you.

@ jimathymonkey

WHEN an American says 'you do the math', you
should probably offer to do the grammar too.

@ Tweeeeed

TOP TIPS FOR LIFE

BECOME the English pop equivalent to
Flo Rida by telling people your new name
is Don Caster or Peter Borough.

@ spudmorrish

PROVE that you had a really great night
out with your friends by uploading
374 photos to Facebook.

@ jayckb

ASTROLOGERS. Avoid criticism of your trade
by writing precise descriptions of future events
instead of the usual old bollocks.

@ jamieohara

PARENTS. Picking up a hitchhiker is a great way to
entertain the kids on long motorway journeys.

@ SteptoeSmith46

CREATE your own cruise ship experience
by visiting an old people's home
whilst sozzled on rum.

@ the_bgr

TWOP TWIPS

INSTANTLY gain hundreds of thousands of Twitter followers by simply becoming a famous actor, singer or sportsperson.

@ somegreybloke

A CONGA is a great way to liven up an otherwise mundane fire drill.

@ madrob1983

IF YOU have a stutter, refrain from saying the word 'ghost'. Otherwise people will think there is one behind them.

@ MatthewRJLogan

D-LIST celebs. If you can't cook, can't dance and don't like jungles, make sure you have a day job to fall back on.

@ jsmithcambr

DON'T have a clock? Simply use scales and slowly pour sand on them. Use a watch and calculator to figure the rest out.

@ lorcychief

CHEER yourself up at the next funeral you go to
by hiding a tenner in your black suit today.

@ DavieLegend

RECREATE a Madonna concert by giving your
nan a leotard and a can of Special Brew.

@ mattie_bennett

TRAIN COMPANIES. Simply suffix your train times
with '-ish' to avoid so many complaints.

@ SpacemanSonic

HIPSTERS. Gain credibility with your pals
by adding 'Sent from my Commodore 64'
to your email signature.

@ Tent101

FOOL colleagues into thinking your email account
has been hacked by sending them 'phishing'
emails at 3am every night.

@ pavanwar

SAVE time opening cards on your birthday
by looking on the back to see what
'the message inside this card says'.

@ dazbradley

TOP TIPS FOR LIFE

AVOID losing your TV remote by sticking it to the television set with a firm adhesive.

@ Castmana1

DEMONSTRATE your intelligence to potential partners by correcting their grammar in social situations.

@ Dr_Draper

TORN UP toilet roll tubes and polystyrene pieces make excellent pot pourri for people with no sense of smell.

@ Nick Motown

SPICE up CVs and covering letters by replacing all full stops with exclamation marks.

@ UWunderkind

OLD JAPANESE MEN. Get teenagers to do your household chores for you by pretending you can teach them karate.

@ GerardTorbitt

TWOP TWIPS

ALWAYS check the Hoover is on before cleaning the house when listening to music on your iPod.

@ Cornishwisdom

FIND your teacher name by putting Mr/Mrs/Miss before your surname.

@ jamieohara

LADIES. Help your future kids remember their passwords by marrying a relative with the same surname as you.

@ Pundamentalism

MINISTERS. Come across as regular guys on the *Today* programme by asking John Humphrys if you 'can say a few hellos'.

@ JonnyB

SINGLE WOMEN. Pretend you are married by filling your bed with farts and toenails.

@ thelucybanks

LOOK UP your partner's name via Google images to see what you could've won.

TWOP TWIPS

PEOPLE who live on roundabouts. Draw less attention to yourselves by drying your 'Happy 40th Kim Taylor' bed linen indoors.

@ GlennyRodge

SPAMMERS. Title your emails 'You've been selected for a reality TV show' to guarantee a population the size of Essex opens it.

@ jojubs

FOOL sexual partners into thinking that you're a driving instructor by slapping the headboard and demanding they stop every now and then.

@ bertnews

PRETEND you're on *The Voice* by having a sing-song next time you're in the queue at the barbers.

@ parkes7

MAKE yourself seem mysterious and exciting by always asking the people you're visiting 'Is there a back way out of here?'

@ MooseAllain

TOP TIPS FOR LIFE

FOOL people into thinking your Shift key isn't
working by typing ;-9 when they give bad news.

@ craiguito

SUBURBAN house owners. Renaming your
semi from 17B to 'The Brambles' transforms
it into a delightful country pile.

@ Johnny_Two_Dogs

SAVE time by brewing all your tea at the start
of the year and then freezing it into 'tea cubes'.
To drink simply microwave.

@ GinBroguesHats

NEW PARENTS. Ensure Facebook friends
recognise you in real life by taping a photo
of your baby over your face.

@ wallaceme

WANT to swim with dolphins but too scared?
Hold two aubergines in the bath;
the texture is very similar.

@ the_overfed

TWOP TWIPS

SAVE the effort of complex Easter egg hunts by simply going to a petrol station where all Easter eggs are clearly displayed.

@ jonculshaw

NAMES of previous sexual partners make ideal 'safe words'.

@ superluckytiger

PENSIONERS. If you haven't got the hang of driving after 50 years, it's probably best to stop driving.

@ 5fendle

RECREATE Simon Cowell's hairstyle by cutting your hair with a knife and fork then brushing it with a toffee apple.

@ MexicanJohn

ENSURE your children's data security by naming their first pet with a mixture of upper and lower case letters and numbers.

@ DanAndDanFilms

IF the grass is greener on the other side, you've laid your turf upside down, you halfwit.

TWOP TWIPS

MUGGERS. Picture yourself in your victims' shoes by stealing their shoes ... and camera phone.

@ aboycalledyoung

HATE your friends? Just reply to their texts with the word 'unsubscribe'; they'll get the hint.

@ kiripritchardmc

HORSES. Fool people into believing you're actually two people in a costume by wearing trainers.

@ John_Joe

ROTARY washing lines make ideal parasols for those that enjoy the sun.

@ Keithbeef007

BANDS. Don't have a pianist? Get on *Later With Jools Holland* and you'll have one play with you whether you want one or not.

@ DavieLegend

TOP TIPS FOR LIFE

ADD variety to your hairdresser's day by
screaming 'Oh God! What have you done?!'
when shown the back of your head.

@ opoint5twins

DISCOVER your porn star name by making
some questionable life choices.

@ iamGusOne

LADIES. Always keep a spare fan-belt in your
handbag, in case your tights snap.

@ TOther_Simon

WIN every argument simply by repeating your
opponent's last sentence in a whiny voice.

@ agqhammond

IN ORDER to get a GP's appointment when you're
feeling unwell, book an appointment one week
before the first symptoms appear.

@ dacy_essex

FIND out how much a woman's clothes cost and the shop they came from by simply mentioning that they look nice.

@ Tomdoerr88

QUICKLY photocopy any important documents before you shred them in case you change your mind later.

@ bobbobob

GIVE your telly that YouTube feel by sellotaping some semi-literate racial abuse to the bottom of the screen.

@ Johnny_Two_Dogs

TURN a boring lasagne into a delicious spaghetti bolognese by simply putting it through a paper shredder.

@ Castmana1

GET THE 'tea tree shower gel' experience by pouring mouthwash over your head and squirting toothpaste in your eyes and arse.

@ hoppythehag

TOP TIPS FOR LIFE

A BIN LINER filled with rubbish
makes a great 'emergency beanbag',
should unwanted guests arrive.

@ Charlieblogger

DON'T anthropomorphise inanimate objects.
They hate it when you do that.

@ PaulOckenden

MEN. Pretend it's Christmas Eve by simply walking
aimlessly around La Senza after 5 pints.

@ JCautomatic

ALWAYS keep a peeled onion next to your
desk so colleagues don't keep questioning
why you are crying at work.

@ TechnicallyRon

MAKE your wife believe you are a
secret agent by only talking to her in
the bathroom with the taps running.

@ matt_h75

THE NEAR DEAD. Cause hilarity at the crematorium by swallowing a handful of popcorn kernels before you go.

@ vinharris

GET a stool in a crowded pub by simply putting Westlife on the jukebox and waiting for the key change.

@ JCautomatic

HAVING an affair? Always meet somewhere people will be too ashamed to say they've seen you. Like Stoke.

@ sixft2blue

CELEBRITIES. Bankrupt a significant portion of the British press by staying at a consistent weight.

@ willrolls

WOMEN. When asked by your husband if you fancy a quickie, understand that he is unlikely to have an alternative option.

@ BigDaddyGrump

TWOP TWIPS

OFFICE WORKERS. Treat every day like a school trip by eating all your sandwiches before 9am and going missing for 3 hours.

@ BigDaddyGrump

AVOID disappointing your parents in later life by showing no promise whatsoever as a child.

@ uselesspostgrad

HOLDING dock leaves over your ears prevents you from hearing Sting's voice.

@ samuelpalin

MAKE neighbours think you have analogue TV by cheering a few seconds before goals are scored in football matches.

@ MushyMelbowHead

DISCOVER if you would enjoy a career as a primary school teacher by reading Amazon product reviews.

@ Dai__Happy

TOP TIPS FOR LIFE

STUBBING your toe while staring in the mirror is an excellent way to preview/ change your 'sex face'.

@ thirsbinamurdir

CHURCH. Make communion more appealing to the younger generation by replacing the wine and bread with WKD and Pringles.

@ rocious_puns

SAVE money on having your portrait painted by committing a terrible crime and having a court artist do it.

@ TweetingTwill

WHY waste money on a potato masher? Simply put the potato in your mouth and chew – hey presto, creamy mash in seconds!

@ hgstevenson

RECREATE a game of Pacman by trying to avoid the salesmen in a furniture store.

@ markb384

TRICK people into thinking that your jumper is a cardigan by gluing buttons or a zip on the front.

@ GinBroguesHats

TURN a quiet country lane into the busiest road in Britain by attempting to have a piss against a hedge alongside it.

@ timcore

PRETEND you've not actually missed your train by crying and waving as it pulls away.

@ bobbobob

CREATE your own Lana Del Rey concert by simply asking any teenager how their day was at school.

@ MesserBest

MAKE your mum think she's at a theme park by handing her your coat and running away.

@ craiguito

SECRET SANTAS. Give your colleague 12 sheets of blank paper and say it's a 2013 Mayan Calendar.

@tomlennon1

TWOP TWIPS

DON'T waste precious hours doing jigsaws.
Buy photographs or paintings instead.

@ tobydavies

HELP compulsive hoarders to 'thin out' their
possessions by introducing them to heroin.

@ vinharris

MEN. Ensure your marriage proposal comes
as a complete surprise by asking your
girlfriend while she's having a poo.

@ fin_oleary

OLD PEOPLE. Stop talking to complete strangers;
everyone hates each other nowadays.

@ StevoGDC

MAKE watching paint dry more interesting
by painting some lovely big tits.

@ _woz_

TOP TIPS FOR LIFE

CONVINCE people you are Derek Acorah by always getting their names wrong with your eyes shut.

@ craiguito

PACIFISTS. Change your surname by deed poll to 'Dancer' to ensure no son of yours ever joins the army.

@ richtextformat

SPICE up a boring salad by replacing the vegetables with bacon and placing it between two slices of bread.

@ RDPursall

PREVENT neighbours from saying 'you can do mine next!' by simply washing every car and mowing every lawn on the street.

@ bored_scientist

ENSURE people visit your grave by having free WiFi installed in it.

@ Skip_Licker

TWOP TWIPS

PHARMACISTS. Pretend to be skilled medical professionals by taking 30 minutes to put a packet of antibiotics in a bag.

@ ILoveGrimsby

TRICK people into thinking you have kids by interrupting your phone conversations with shouts of 'stop it' and 'put that down'.

@ I_am_Lukem

CHRIS REA. By switching jobs to work closer to home you may avoid having to start driving so early each December.

@ JonnyB

GET away with being caught by a speed camera by getting a passenger to hold a gun to your head.

@ Woof_the_wolf

ITV. Make an ITV1-1 channel. Why should it just be tardy people who benefit from the digital age?

@ loop_deleted

CONVINCE your neighbour you've gone senile by knocking on his door and asking if he wants to come out to play.

@ rowzed

TWOP TWIPS

CONVINCE people you are a cat by staring
at them with literally no emotion on your
face before licking your genitals.

@ BigDaddyGrump

PRETEND that you're Jamie Oliver by referring
to a humble roast potato as a 'bad boy'.

@ jayckb

STOP delicious fat from running out of your
meat by placing a book under the front legs
of your George Foreman grill.

@ parkes7

SAVE precious time flossing your teeth every
morning by having them grouted.

@ delrico

ACUPUNCTURISTS. Ensure a loyal customer
base by putting a bit of heroin on the
end of your needles.

@ SaliBerisha1

TOP TIPS FOR LIFE

GET AN Australian to tell you how much
better they do things 'back home' by
simply talking to him.

@ moanup

EASILY collect spilled dry Sugar Puffs by
carefully walking on them in socks.

@ gdorean

INSOMNIACS. Have you tried having a full
Christmas dinner then watching a recording of the
Queen's Christmas speech before bedtime?

@ DeKuipo2

SAVE time when saying 'ham sandwich' by simply
saying 'hamwich'. (Also works with jam.)

@ PeasOneDay

UNI STUDENTS. Reduce the chances of
flatmates stealing your food by 50% by covering
everything in your fridge with Marmite.

@ andiejae

TWOP TWIPS

SAVE TIME and money by not texting
in to breakfast radio to tell them what
you're doing today. No one cares.

@ dvdmcn

JEREMY KYLE guests. Pay for your own
DNA tests by saving up all the money
you get from the tooth fairy.

@ silentglen

FOOL the kids into thinking this will be
the best Xmas ever by circling all the
expensive stuff in the Argos catalogue.

@ bingowings14

PRETEND you're my neighbour by borrowing
my tools for weeks at a time and sleeping
with my wife when I'm at work.

@ ben_cameron

COUNCILS. Save money on expensive lollipop
ladies and reduce risk to children by building
schools on the other side of the road.

@ daryllayton

OLD LADIES. Want a cup of tea and someone to listen to you? Try shoplifting.

TWOP TWIPS

DOCTORS. Relax men undergoing a
prostate exam by putting on a Barry White CD
just as you're about to begin.

@ NickMotown

MEN. Help hold that bath towel up by
showering in false breasts.

@ Splats

FETISHISTS. Instead of joining Uniform
Dating, meet the hunks of your dreams by
committing crimes while on fire.

@ wallaceme

KIDS. Simply move all your favourite toys
to the naughty step just before you feel
a tantrum coming on.

@ scottywrotem

MAKE your neighbour think that he's been in a
coma by putting hundreds of full milk bottles
outside his house one night.

@ Pundamentalism

TOP TIPS FOR LIFE

Parents. Don't have a pumpkin for Halloween?
Just apply fake tan to a football.

@ TonyCowards

MAKE your own electric toothbrush by simply
gaffer-taping an ordinary toothbrush to a vibrator.

@ kentjack

HOME-WORKERS. Don't bother buying Christmas
presents. Just wait for the postman to bring your
neighbours' parcels to you instead.

@ FunkyMagic

REPLICATE the feeling of taking
holiday snaps with an iPad by eating
a trifle with a garden trowel.

@ jamesjgalbraith

FAMILIES. Fancy a nice leisurely Sunday
afternoon stroll? Go to the park or
the woods, NOT ASDA.

@ RachJBurns

TWOP TWIPS

STOP children playing with your stuff
by saying it belongs to them.

@ orangeaurochs

FOOL neighbours into thinking that Ninja Turtles
have moved into your street by having pizzas
delivered to the nearest drain.

@ Hend017

PRETEND you're on *Million Pound Drop* by
asking your wife multiple choice questions
then flushing her purse down the toilet.

@ saladwhipperjim

MAKE YOUR one night stand feel much better by
leaving them a few quid on the bedside table.

@ missspellbound

GIVE your cat the experience of being
born again by lining the inside edges
of its cat flap with wafer thin ham.

@ death_stairs

JEALOUS that you're missing out on the flirty camaraderie of your smoking friends at the pub? Simply pop out for a fart instead.

@AbbeyBloom

DAVID DICKINSON. Now is the time of year to sand yourself down, apply a new coat of stain and stand in the shed until April.

@ Rusty_Ricker

ENLIVEN your bank statements by getting your friends and family to label any transfers 'sex boat trip' or 'armed heist cut'.

@ russellpeake

TEACHERS. Pretend you're hosting *Question Time* by referring to kids with their hand up as 'the child in the white shirt'.

@ thenumbersong

THIRSTY people. Confuse your throat by drinking cranberry juice.

@ MesserBest

GIVE someone who does tireless work in your community a surprise by taking them to see *Surprise Surprise* but not surprising them.

@ _Enanem_

TOP TIPS FOR LIFE

AVOID the inconvenience of opening
and closing baby gates by installing a
cattle grid at the top of the stairs.

@ BobWriggles

COSMETIC COMPANIES. Instead of testing
make-up on animals, use Photoshop to
get an idea of what they'd look like.

@ craiguito

AMAZE Bruce Springsteen by using a
magnifying glass on a sunny day to
start a fire without a spark.

@ This_Is_Kit

MEN OVER 35. Save money on expensive
alarm clocks by simply drinking a glass
of water before you go to bed.

@ pfon73

CELEBRATE the end of Stoptober by treating
yourself to a packet of fags.

@ mikeycurtis

WHEN giving directions, make people think
they're in a horror movie by telling a short
sinister story about their destination.

@ JCbeermat

DROPPED your phone into some rice? Don't worry,
just leave it in a bowl of water overnight.

@ graham_r_miller

ENSURE a regular source of good luck by feeding
your dog pennies before taking it for a walk.

@ S_Gresham

MEN. Make it a Valentine's Day she'll always
remember by simply forgetting it.

@ a_stoth

WOMEN. Don't sell seashells on the seashore.
Boost profits by selling them somewhere
they are less readily available.

@ njllewy

PREPARE for Christmas early by falling out with relatives now.

@ AbbeyBloom

BY repeatedly throwing your toddler in the
air you can easily convince neighbours
that you've got a trampoline.
@ JWilliamsRacing

PARENTS. An old baby bottle makes a splendid
measuring cup for spirits. Remember to rinse
before the health visitor comes.
@ cakepopprincess

CADBURY'S Miniature Heroes make
convenient suppositories for those
too busy to take a full bar orally.
@ SteKelly

COUPLES. Add a frantic urgency to your
lovemaking by hiring Richard O'Brien to lounge
outside your bedroom playing the harmonica.
@ Brainmage

IMPROVE office communication by
shouting 'I've just sent you an email' every
time you send someone an email.
@ freethestones

TOP TIPS FOR LIFE

ADD model ruins, aquatic plants and goldfish
to your toilet bowl to make an unattractive
domestic feature really rather pretty.

@ RippoJMan

PRETEND you're a cat by tripping your
wife up when you're hungry.

@ paulkelly2007

FOOL colleagues into thinking you are working
hard by simply lowering the knot in your tie.

@ chuddsy92

EASILY identify who's constantly stinking
out the office toilets by swapping the
air-freshener for an air-horn.

@ vinharris

WATCH STOMP for free by telling your
binmen to bugger off.

@ SteptoeSmith46

BECOME the office printer jam expert by simply having your desk right next to a printer.

@ DanPeroni

PHARMACISTS. Stop people obtaining medicine fraudulently by making them memorise the first line of an address.

@ dacy_essex

EARPHONES playing drum 'n' bass music make ideal defibrillators for mice.

@ PeteJScott

CONTRACT WRITERS. Dot the 'i's & cross the 't's as you go to save valuable time going through it all again at the end.

@ td_ward

FRIEND HAD A BABY? Share in their wonder, joy and boundless love by clicking 'Like' on Facebook.

@ willrolls

PRISON GOVERNORS. Increase inmate morale by pretending they are on a luxury cruise.

@ TomCullen

TWOP TWIPS

SAVE money on expensive Valentine's gifts by erecting emotional barriers all around you and growing old and dying alone.

@ TweetCashmore

TEENAGERS. Ensure you demand a refund from the cinema if the film distracts you from your phone.

@ SandyFootwells

TO DISCOVER lots of features that you never knew existed on your PC, simply ask your cat to walk across your keyboard.

@ Bruno_Di_Gradi

RECREATE the thrill of writing a blog by screaming your deepest, most profound thoughts into the dark, uncaring, night sky.

@ ChribHibble

CONVINCE people you're always winning at tombolas by sticking raffle tickets to the top of every tin and jar in your cupboard.

@ Oak411

TOP TIPS FOR LIFE

MARK the protracted suffering and death
on the cross of Our Lord Jesus Christ by
eating mildly spiced fruit buns.

@ orangeaurochs

PRETEND your family loves you by putting
'dreading work' on Facebook on Sunday night.

@ Swissss

ENSURE your kids stay in bed at night by
standing at their door in a clown mask
with plastic cutlery taped to your fingers.

@ death_stairs

FACEBOOKERS. Save time in restaurants by asking
for a meal that's already been Instagrammed.

@ vinharris

TEACH your kids that life is not all about
having fun by taking them to see
an Adam Sandler comedy.

@ Dai__Happy

TWOP TWIPS

KIDS. Treat your parents' house like
a hotel by reviewing it on Trip Advisor
and stealing all the shampoo.

@ GinBroguesHats

FREAK out a budgie-owning friend
by placing a Cadbury's Mini Egg in the
cage when they aren't looking.

@ Bloddys_world

MAKE your mum believe you're a successful jet-
setter by arranging to call her at '7pm your time'.

@ AdamF_

PRETEND you are a time-traveller by asking
people the year, then whooping for joy and
shouting 'IT BLOODY WORKED!!'

@ vinharris

CONDOMS make excellent 'wellies' for cats.

@ OwenDixon9

@ H20_2011

BECOMING a parent is a great time to quit smoking/reading/sleeping/ leaving the house after 6pm.

@ cambridgeblue10

CANCEL out a receding hairline by constantly raising your eyebrows.

@ neillockwood

SAVE time and money on costly de-icer and simply drive your vehicle with your head out of the window like a happy dog.

@ piphunter81

DOUBLE the battery life of an iPhone by putting the bloody thing down.

@ steve_stringer

GET the *Saturday Kitchen* experience at home by drinking a glass of Shiraz with your cornflakes.

@ MrAGriffiths

TOP TIPS FOR LIFE

SAVE MONEY on expensive spectacles by memorising the last two lines of the optician's chart: KHUYBN and FTERXCL.

@ hewnique

WAKE up your baby by gently resting your head on a pillow.

@ RobinsonS

SHEPHERDS. Remain conscious during a stock-take by thinking of a concern then turning it over and over in your mind.

@ Johnny_Two_Dogs

GORDON RAMSAY. Save thousands of pounds on expensive Botox by grouting your face with Princes Beef Paste.

@ buschenfeld

BLOOD ORANGES are a healthy alternative for squeamish vampires.

@ shefskip

WORK from home? Shred your documents at 3am with the lights off to give mundane chores an exciting Watergate vibe.

@ mant_a_tangi

SAVE time in the mornings by taking a mug and tea bag into the shower.

@ zeenat_sal

REGISTER with Groupon if you too enjoy deleting eight emails every morning.

@ TheCoester

UP AND COMING bands. Get free advertising by calling yourselves Missing Cat.

@ Thekjhandbook

RECREATE the Superbowl experience of staying up all night staring at something you barely understand by having a baby.

@ tweetymactweeto

SINGLES. Avoid feeling so lonely by
waving at yourself in the mirror while
brushing your teeth.

TWOP TWIPS

IF YOU suspect a policeman to be a ghost, throw a
rock at him. If he is it will pass straight through.

@ rlindley85

TUNA FISH. Avoid ending up in a tin
by being 'unfriendly' to dolphins.

@ OwenDixon9

COUPLES. A Valentine's Day dinner out is
an excellent way to maintain your bleak
charade of love and happiness.

@ richtextformat

BEFORE swimming, test your lifeguard's
credentials by pushing him into the water.

@ ehdannyboy

ENSURE your horse falls horribly and
gets shot at this year's Grand National by
letting your children pick out the name.

@ southeastbint

TOP TIPS FOR LIFE

ELDERLY MEN. Give yourself an air of Hugh Hefner by referring to your carers as 'playmates'.

@ craiguito

AVOID answering difficult questions in meetings by shouting 'RELEASE THE BEES' into your watch and running out the door.

@ pacific_amnesia

TO FIND OUT how long a piece of string is, pull it straight and measure the distance between the ends.

@ SteveSparshott

CAN'T WAIT for the next episode of *Game Of Thrones*? Simply flick between a *Lord Of The Rings* DVD and the adult channels.

@ Castmana1

WRITE the alphabet around the edge of your ironing board to encourage ghosts to do the work for you.

@ GrahamGoring

TWOP TWIPS

SAVE money on a Halloween party for your kids by simply taking them to Wetherspoon's for their tea.

@ JCautomatic

RECREATE the joy of having a teenage son by moving an orang-utan into your house and teaching it to play Call Of Duty.

@ OwenDixon9

MISS the 'Dial-A-Disc' service? Simply phone British Gas and select Option 1 – Emergencies.

@ paininthebrum

RECREATE those hedonistic party days in Ibiza by standing up a bit too quickly.

@ _TomMcLaughlin

CALCULATE how many people live in your house by dividing the total number of pairs of 3D glasses in your home by 12.

@ TheCoester

TOP TIPS FOR LIFE

TEACHERS. Why not have a training day
where you learn to drive in snow?

@ JCautomatic

ACUPUNCTURISTS. Save the hassle of
travelling to work each day by 'remote
working' using voodoo dolls.

@ Dai__Happy

GIVE your wife a bag of potpourri for Valentine's
Day and tell her it's a bunch of roses jigsaw.

@ JonS1950

MEN. Convince people you have a massive
penis by driving very considerately
in a modest family saloon car.

@ MooseAllain

WATCH a complete stranger's child grow bigger
by the day by creating a Facebook account.

@ pavanwar

COUNCILLORS. Avoid being mistaken for counsellors by making it clear you don't care about people or their problems.

@ Cain_Unable

IF A GENIE won't let you wish for more wishes, wish for a second, less restrictive genie.

@ JonasPolsky

GRANDPARENTS. Create a party atmosphere over Xmas dinner by talking about medical procedures and updating us on local deaths.

@ 664NOTB

COTTON BUDS make ideal toothpicks for Health and Safety officers.

@ vinharris

A WASPS' nest makes an excellent piñata for masochists.

@ Castmana1

PRETEND to be a smartphone owner by randomly staring at an upheld bar of chocolate.

@ new_toon

TWOP TWIPS

DOG WALKERS. Avoid being mugged by putting all your valuables in a small black plastic bag.

@ TonyCowards

PUT YOUR socks in a room with a bottle of wine, a bowl of Twiglets and a Dido album and they'll match themselves eventually.

@ GlennyRodge

IMPROVE any Mumford & Sons song by slowing it down 100%.

@ Thumbsuk

ADD a touch of regality to your poos by holding the toilet brush and wearing your shower cap.

@ pavanwar

MAKE the game Operation more realistic by telling your kids they've got it for Xmas but not letting them have it till August.

@ JCautomatic

TOP TIPS FOR LIFE

ALLERGY SUFFERERS. Experience the joys of
pet ownership by paying an ungrateful friend's
food bill and cleaning up their faeces.

@ JoelGodfrey

PARENTS. Avoid the monotony of the
school run by dropping your child off
at a different school each day.

@ DanPeroni

TEACH mime artists not to cry wolf
by locking them in a greenhouse.

@ tommycrumples

FOOL neighbours into believing you're invisible
by stiffening your dog's lead with starch and
sending him out for a walk on his own.

@ MatCro

STOP your kids having nightmares about a
monster under the bed by explaining it's
been eaten by the clown in the loft.

@ buschenfeld

BECOME a successful celebrity lookalike
by becoming famous and then
pretending not to be you.

@ BisleyT

CONVINCE your wife you've been looking at
porn by throwing your laptop out of the window
as soon as she walks in the room.

@ shippingorder

FUN GAME. Ride a bicycle with an empty baby
seat down a busy street whilst loudly saying,
'You're being VERY well behaved.'

@ ChribHibble

JUST before you go to sleep, quietly slip
on a clown mask just in case your partner
wakes in the night with hiccups.

@ ehdannyboy

LEARN *everything* about Moshi Monsters by
simply having unprotected sex 6 years ago.

@ Swissss

SUPERGLUE and a firm handshake will ensure you're always remembered after job interviews.

@ tokyo_sexwhale

TWOP TWIPS

AS cinemas are so frightfully loud
these days, make sure your ringtone
volume is turned all the way up.

@ orangeaurochs

TIRED of being single? Want to know the secret
of success? Lower your standards. A lot.

@ Jeffwni

A SMALL coniferous tree in the corner of your
living room is an excellent space to store
Christmas decorations.

@ drifterpowell

PLAY a real-life game of Guess Who by asking your
wife if she has a beard before pushing her over.

@ PalmHerNova

RECREATE the joy of applying sun cream
to a child by trying to gift wrap a shark.

@ andrewb1970

TOP TIPS FOR LIFE

FOOL the window cleaner into thinking he's
got no clothes on by standing naked on the
other side of the glass and copying him.

@ guy_parsons

LOOK slimmer in time for summer by spiking
your partner's food with weight gain powder.

@ SimEditorial

ENJOY the sophisticated ambience of
a sushi bar by strapping some peeled
fish fingers to a Scalextric car.

@ MarionDowling

TRICK work colleagues into thinking that you've
had an affair by cutting the arms off all your suits.

@ mantropik

PRETEND you're a twin by climbing out of the
bathroom window, ringing the doorbell and
asking your wife if she's seen your twin.

@ ScottHoad

GIVE your kitchen a relaxed gastropub vibe by writing numbers on your kitchen utensils.

@ Polly_Graph

CHANNEL 5. Cash in on confused gift-buyers this Christmas by releasing your own perfume.

@ sixft2blue

MAKE new friends by pretending to be interested in other people's lives.

@ thisisnotally

PRETEND to be a dad walking his son to school by shouting 'COME ON' 47 times at a snail.

@ milesorru

MAKE your friends feel like they're old and uncool by ending texts with the letters from your postcode FTL!

@ PaulJames43

AVOID repetitive strain injury by never doing anything more than once.

B ∃ C K

@_b_4

TWOP TWIPS

ENCOURAGE a strike in your workplace by
lighting a fire in an oil drum in the staff car park.

@ dannysutcliffes

SHOW your crying child their birth video
in reverse and tell them that's what happens
to kids who don't stop crying.

@ Thekjhandbook

LONELY PEOPLE. Make yourself think you
had a big night out by hiding a naked stranger
under the duvet before going to bed.

@ MarionDowling

SAVE money on the expensive Grand Theft
Auto computer game simply by moving to
Wythenshawe and doing your best to 'fit in'.

@ StockportRed

BUSINESSMEN. Make people think you
have a private helicopter by arriving
for meetings three hours too early.

@ SJBerrington

TOP TIPS FOR LIFE

A MAGPIE glued to the end of a broom handle
makes an excellent organic metal detector.

@ TOther_Simon

DRIVERS. Alleviate the embarrassment of
accidentally stopping in a box junction
by hiding in the footwell.

@ DoccerP

PRETEND you work in Greggs by staring blankly
each time someone says, 'Sausage roll, please.'

@ gdorean

A SIMPLE TRICK for calculating 'dog years'
is to count the number of iPad launches
since a puppy's birth.

@ willrolls

NON-SMOKERS. Don't miss out on the
social ice-breaker of asking for a light by
carrying around a box of sparklers.

@ TeaAndCopy

TWOP TWIPS

FIND out if you like pies by asking a friend
to hold one under your chins.

@ Thumbsuk

CAN'T be bothered to Google your illness?
Just go to your GP who will do it for you.

@ Instinctivetip

FAST-TRACK your way to becoming a mafia boss
by changing your first name to Don.

@ philswales

AIM for maximum awkwardness at the
wedding of an ex-boyfriend by turning
up in the same dress as the bride.

@ RaisingEdgar

ONESIE WEARERS. Avoid chilly nudity when
having a poo by simply cutting it at waist level
into easy top and bottom sections.

@ misstoogood

TOP TIPS FOR LIFE

CLINGFILM makes an ideal substitute for
wrapping paper when wrapping presents for
people who hate surprises.

@ charliesarson

GIVE geeks a panic attack by sitting
in a deckchair with a Thermos outside
an Apple store at midnight.

@ Midgetgems26

WHEN skydiving, don't pull the ripcord until 3ft
from the ground. That way, if the parachute
fails, you haven't got far to fall.

@ Ginja_Mick

BECOME 'An absolutely superb eBayer!' by simply
buying something and then paying for it.

@ cluedont

IF ASKED in a job interview to describe
yourself in three words why not try
'violent when disappointed'?

@ acsdawson

TWOP TWIPS

MAKE perfect scrambled eggs by starting out
with the intention of making an omelette.

@ dan_shirley88

CALL OF DUTY gamers. Re-enact a World War I
Christmas by switching to FIFA13 to play a
friendly against Germany in Belgium.

@ MoZZMAN

MAN UTD FANS. Make your own
Alex Ferguson snowman by replacing
the traditional carrot with a raspberry.

@ mothmun

PRETEND to be a rapper by asking
ladies in bikinis what your name is.

@ trouteyes

TOO busy to check Facebook?
Your friends have babies, cats, cupcakes
and dubious politics. You're welcome.

@ BigRedTone

TRAVEL on the train for free by
disdainfully wheeling around a trolley
of warm kit-kats and inedible pasties.

B ⱻ c K

@ Johnny_Two_Dogs

TWOP TWIPS

CONVEY your dissatisfaction at any situation by appearing in the local paper with your arms folded.

@ themightyjose

CHEFS. Spaghetti hoops placed by the hob could be the difference between life and death for any flies in your soup.

@ alienonline

WORRIED MEN. Always arrange your VD check-up for Feb 14; you can safely put it on the kitchen calendar then.

@ vinharris

BALD PEOPLE. Tattoo a line across your forehead so you know when to stop when washing your face.

@ Bigshirtlesscol

AVOID wasting your life in bookshops by judging a book by its cover.

@ RobMcGarr

TOP TIPS FOR LIFE

AMBULANCE DRIVERS. To avoid rushing about and making a noise simply start your journeys 10 minutes earlier.

@ PhilipIndigo

IF YOUR phone runs out of battery on the train simply distribute a brief autobiography to all nearby passengers.

@ thewritertype

PARENTS. Save money on expensive clothes for growing kids by buying them cigarettes instead.

@ TheBathBird

KEEPING pets indoors on November 5th doesn't mean they have to miss the family fun: simply get them some indoor fireworks.

@ kevinmarkwick

MAKE horses think they're going to prison by taking pictures of them in their horseboxes.

@ MrMichaelSpicer

RETAILERS. 'Gift ideas' is a great euphemism for 'things people would never buy for themselves'.

@ peterajackson

A CARROT wrapped in lettuce makes an ideal vegetarian pig in a blanket.

@ RANTINGMALE

GUYS. Liven up your Friday by accidentally texting the wife: 'Simon, we'll have a proper Valentine's next year, I promise.'

@ bobbobob

EMULATE Jesus this Easter by deactivating your Facebook profile on Friday and reactivating it Sunday morning.

@peter_brush

TEST R KELLY'S ability to fly by pushing him out of a window.

@ MetalOllie

TUNNELLING under your neighbour's house may
take months of effort, but imagine their
faces when you surface in their living room.

@5fendle

TWOP TWIPS

TRICK YOUR CAR into thinking it's put on
weight by driving it with the handbrake on.

@moanup

ENCOURAGE your cat to live a more active life by
telling it that it died peacefully 8 times in its sleep.

@ Johnny_Two_Dogs

GLUE SNIFFERS. Gently wean yourself off your
habit by sticking pieces of sellotape to your arm.

@comedyfish

TWO USED toilet roll holders taped together
make ideal binoculars for viewing objects
that require no magnification.

@ srafferty73

RESPECT the elderly by bumping fists with
them as you pass on the street.

@ jac_bond

TOP TIPS FOR LIFE

CONVINCE OTHERS you're full of great ideas
by gluing a light bulb to the top of your head.

@ mothmum

ATTRACT women with colds by wearing
Vicks VapoRub instead of aftershave.

@ Birdflaps

RECREATE that 'large print' experience with your
audiobooks by simply turning up the volume.

@manfrommandm

CELEBRATE Friday 13th by finding superstitious
people and tripping them over.

@missnpatel

DISTRACT yourself from post-holiday
blues by counting the number of working
hours you have before retirement.

@ pfon73

SUDOKU puzzles make great painting by numbers gifts for aspiring Cubists.

@ AbeMitchell

TEASE violent muggers by wearing headphones down dark alleyways but having no iPod for them to steal.

@ welshboymick

PRETEND you're a professional tennis player by wiping your face on a towel every 30 seconds then throwing it at a child.

@ _b_4

CALL CENTRES. If at all times you're 'experiencing an unexpectedly high volume of calls', you should raise your expectations.

@ christof_ff

DIETERS. Give yourself the illusion of having just finished a whole curry by eating a single mint imperial off an ashtray.

@ joewellscomic

TOP TIPS FOR LIFE

DOG OWNERS. Ensure your dog always comes back by shortening both legs on one side.

@ vinharris

A MICROWAVE oven makes an ideal TV for people who just like watching cookery programmes.

@ wbowman73

PARENTS. Save the hassle of writing your child's name on their school clothes by calling your son George and shopping at Asda.

@ jcolls

SAVE money on new shoes for your kids by forcing them to stay at the fish pedicure spa until their old shoes fit again.

@ MrLemonDrizzle

AUTHORS. Finish every sentence of your book with either a sad or happy face, to give younger readers an indication of mood.

@ ponceywoncey

acknowledgements

Grateful thanks to my agent James Wills
and to BeCK for his marvellous illustrations
(you can see more of his work by following
him on Twitter: @ new_toon).

Thanks to my wife Lisa, Mam, Dad,
family and friends.

And cheers to my Twitter followers.